CAMERON MACKINTOSH PRESENTS

BOUBLIL & SCHÖNBERG'S

Miss Saigon

A MUSICAL BY
ALAIN BOUBLIL & CLAUDE-MICHEL SCHÖNBERG

PRODUCTION CREDITS FROM THE FIRST LONDON PRODUCTION:

Music by **CLAUDE-MICHEL SCHÖNBERG**
Lyrics by **RICHARD MALTBY, JR. & ALAIN BOUBLIL**
Adapted from the original French lyrics by **ALAIN BOUBLIL**
Additional material by **RICHARD MALTBY, JR.**

Musical supervision by **DAVID CADDICK & MARTIN KOCH**
Directed by **NICHOLAS HYTNER**
Musical staging by **BOB AVIAN**
Production designed by **JOHN NAPIER**
Costumes designed by **ANDREANE NEOFITOU**
Lighting by **DAVID HERSEY**
Sound by **ANDREW BRUCE**
Orchestration by **WILLIAM D. BROHN**

World première: Miss Saigon opened at the
Theatre Royal, Drury Lane on 20th September 1989

Exclusive distributors
Music Sales Limited
8/9 Frith Street, London W1D 3JB, England.
Music Sales Pty Limited
120 Rothschild Avenue, Rosebery, NSW 2018, Australia.

'This photograph was for Alain and I the start of everything...'

Claude-Michel Schönberg, October 1985

'The heat is on in Saigon
the girls are hotter 'n hell.'

MISS Saigon

This book © Copyright 1990.
Order No. MF10044 ISBN 0.7119.2208.X

Rights of dramatic performance for all countries of
the world administered by
Cameron Mackintosh Limited,
1 Bedford Square, London WC1B 3RA.
Telephone: 020 7637 8866. Telex: 226164 (CAMACK)
Fax: 020 7436 2683.

Print rights for the United Kingdom & Eire administered by
Music Sales Limited, 8/9 Frith Street, London W1D 3JB.
Telephone: 020 7434 0066. Fax: 020 7439 2848.

Photography by Michael Le Poer Trench.
Music arranged by Tony Castro.
Music processed by Barnes Music Engraving.
Cover & logo device design by Dewynters plc.
Cover design Copyright © by Cameron Mackintosh Limited.
Book design by Mike Bell.
Typeset by Capital Setters.
Printed in Great Britain.

'I have a heart like the sea
a million dreams are in me.'

'I'm from a world that's so different
from all that you are
how in the light of one night
did we come so far?'

'In a place that won't let us feel
in a life where nothing seems real
I have found you.'

'This room! This shame
will haunt you while you live.'

'I have killed with this hand,
I have killed oh why am I cold?
For this must be a judgement fulfilled'.

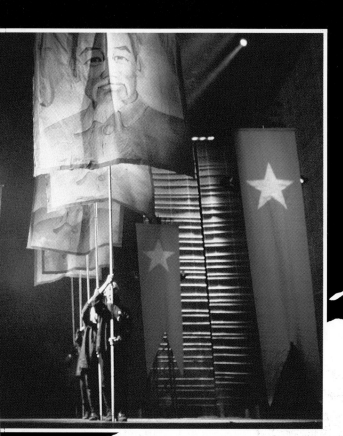

'They're called Bui-doi, the dust of life
conceived in hell and born in strife.'

'We can't forget, must not forget
that they are all our children too.'

'They'll kill who they find here
don't leave us behind here.'

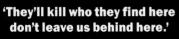

'What's that I smell in the air?
The American dream.'

'As long as you can have your chance
I swear I'll give my life for you.'

The Heat Is On In Saigon

Music by Claude-Michel Schönberg
Lyrics by Richard Maltby Jr. & Alain Boublil
Adapted from original French Lyrics by Alain Boublil

The heat is on in Sai-gon___ the girls are hot-ter 'n Hell

one of these slits here will be Miss Sai-gon God the ten-sion is high

_ not to men-tion the smell _   The heat is on in Sai-gon _ Is there a war go-ing on?

Don't ask I ain't gon-na tell _____

How are you do-ing there John?

I got the hots for Y-vonne

I tell you Bud-dy   I've had it   I don't want to hear

We should get drunk and get laid — since the end is so near —

The heat is on in Sai-gon — but 'til they tell me I'm gone — I'm gon-na buy you a   girl

You can buy me a beer

gently

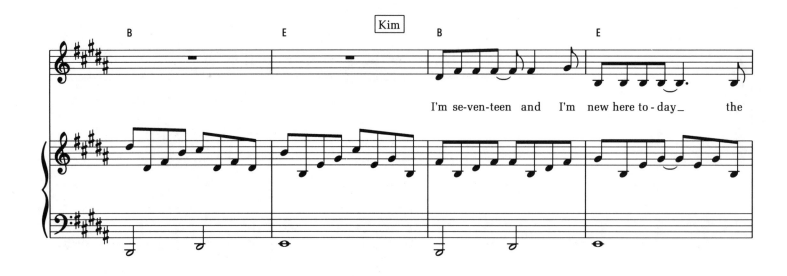

I'm se-ven-teen and I'm new here to-day— the

vil-lage I come— from seems so far a-way— All of the girls— know much

more what to say— but I know I have a heart like the sea—— A mil-lion dreams are in me

Good Je-sus John who is she?

The Cong is tight-'ning the noose___   Is it a week or a day   or an hour that we get?

to-night could be our last shot   got to put it to use

to-night I bet that you and I will get a - long. For-get a-bout the threat for - get the Vi - et - cong

Mi - mi Gi - gi Y - vette or Y - vonne_____ Gon - na buy me a beer

__ and e - lect Miss Sai - gon

(Engineer: Attention s'il vous plaît! By popular

demand, Miss Gigi Van Tranh, is crowned Miss Saigon!)   The heat is on in Sai-gon

and things are not go-ing well   but still at mid-night   the par-ty goes on __

a good-bye par-ty in hell _____

The Movie In My Mind

Music by Claude-Michel Schönberg
Lyrics by Richard Maltby Jr. & Alain Boublil
Adapted from original French Lyrics by Alain Boublil

Why God Why?

Music by Claude-Michel Schönberg
Lyrics by Richard Maltby Jr. & Alain Boublil
Adapted from original French Lyrics by Alain Boublil

Why does Sai-gon ne-ver sleep at night?

Why does this girl smell of o-range trees? How can I feel good when no-thing's right?

Why is she cool when there is no breeze? Vi - et - nam. You don't give an-swers do you

When I went home be - fore____ no - one talked of the war.____ What they knew from T. V.____

____ did-n't have a thing to do with me.____

I went back and re - upped,____ sure Sai - gon is cor - rupt.____ It felt bet - ter to be____

here dri - ving for the Em - bas - sy.

'Cos here__ if you can pull a string a guy__ like me

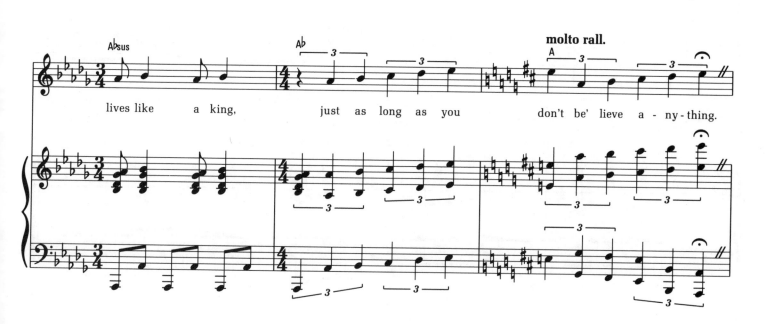

lives like a king, just as long as you don't be' lieve a - ny - thing.

very gentle

Why God? Why this face? Why such beau-ty____ in this place? I liked my mem'-ries as they were but now I'll leave re-mem-b'ring her, just her.____

Sun And Moon

Music by Claude-Michel Schönberg
Lyrics by Richard Maltby Jr. & Alain Boublil
Adapted from original French Lyrics by Alain Boublil

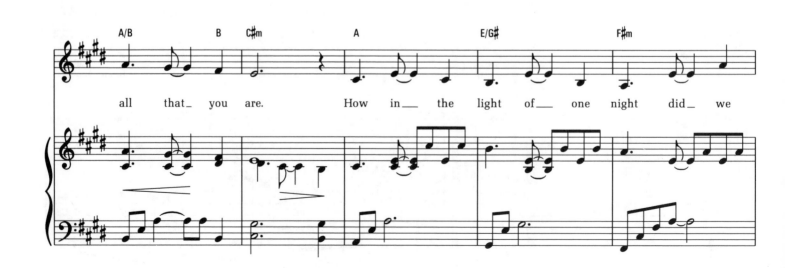

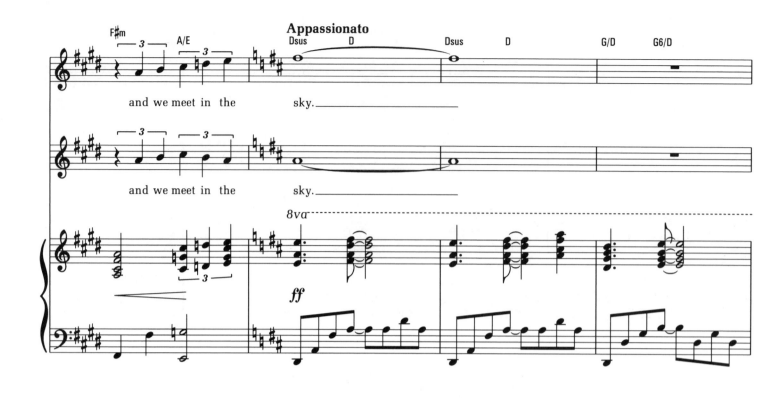

and we meet in the sky._____

and we meet in the sky._____

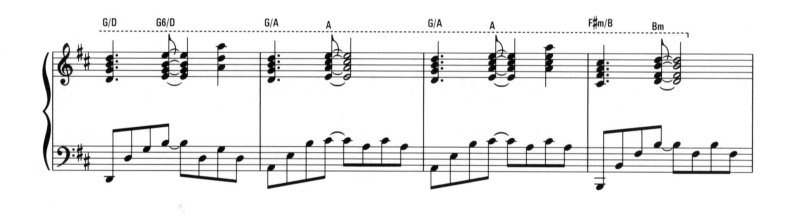

a tempo tranquillo

You are— sun - light and I moon joined here—

bright - 'ning the sky with the flame of love.

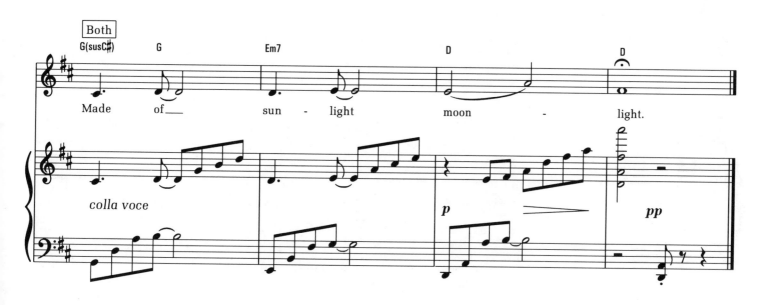

Made of— sun - light moon - light.

The Last Night Of The World

Music by Claude-Michel Schönberg
Lyrics by Richard Maltby Jr. & Alain Boublil
Adapted from original French Lyrics by Alain Boublil

Languidly

Chris

In a place that won't let us feel.____ In a life where no-thing seems real,

I have found you. I have found you.____

On the o-ther side of the Earth,___ there's a place where life still has worth.

___ I will take you. I'll go with you._____ You won't be -

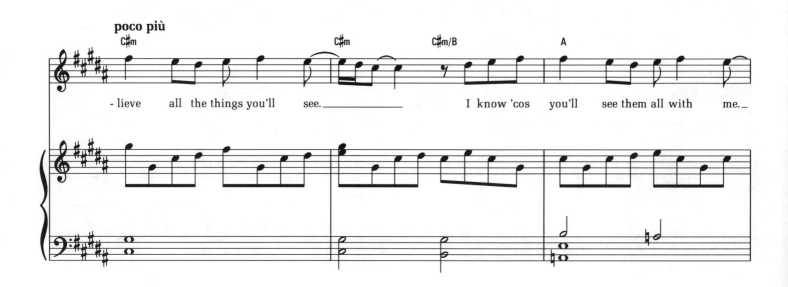

- lieve all the things you'll see._____ I know 'cos you'll see them all with me.___

If we're to - ge - ther, well then, we'll hear it a - gain. A

If we're to - ge - ther, well then, we'll hear it a - gain. A

song played on a so - lo sax - o - phone,___ a

song played on a so - lo sax - o - phone,___ a

cra - zy sound. A lone - ly sound, a cry that tells us love___ goes on and on.

cra - zy sound. A lone - ly sound, a cry that tells us love___ goes on and on.

So stay with me and hold me tight and dance, like it's the

So stay with me and hold me tight and dance, like it's the

last night of the world.

last night of the world.

I Still Believe

Music by Claude-Michel Schönberg
Lyrics by Richard Maltby Jr. & Alain Boublil
Adapted from original French Lyrics by Alain Boublil

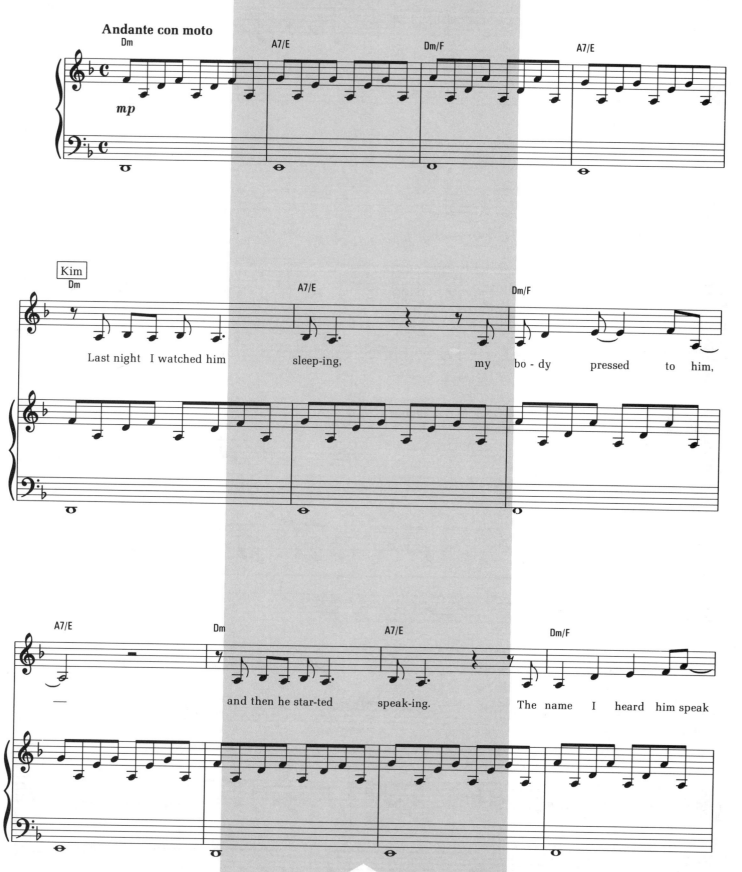

Last night I watched him sleep-ing, my bo-dy pressed to him,

— and then he star-ted speak-ing. The name I heard him speak

It's all o-ver, I'm here, there is no-thing to fear.   Chris, what's haunt - ing

you?   Can't you let me in - side what you so want to

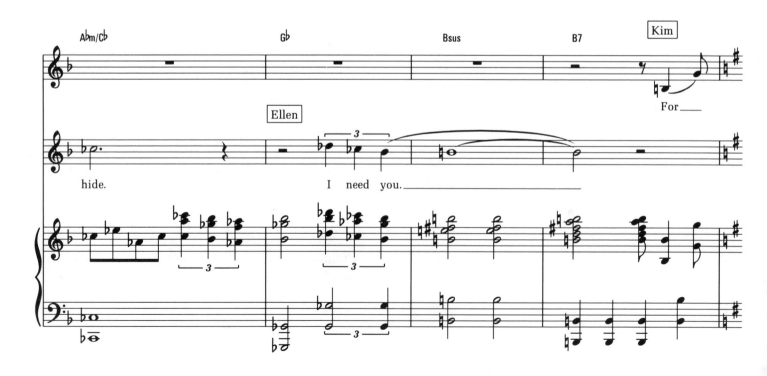

hide.   I need you.   For___

Ellen   Kim

and I know why. I'm yours un - til we die.

I'm your wife now, for life, un - til we die.

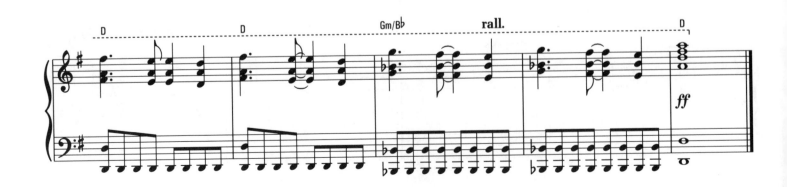

If You Want To Die In Bed

Music by Claude-Michel Schönberg
Lyrics by Richard Maltby Jr. & Alain Boublil
Adapted from original French Lyrics by Alain Boublil

If you want to die in bed, fol - low my ex - am - ple.

When you see a cloud a - head, it's time__ to show your class.

Hit the door be - fore____ they make a tar-get of your ass.

If you want to die in bed in times of rev - o - lu-tion,

when the flag they wave is red, let pride_ fill up your chest.

Mean-while pack a sack,____ and take the first boat head-ing

west.

My pre-cious sou-ve-nirs of all____ the gol-den years.

Ro-lex wat-ches in steel____ that look prac-tic-'lly real.____

Leggiero, meno mosso

Grab a stash of cash___ and plan a rest-'rant in the States.

Let me stop for a bit. This was___ my great-est hit.

Miss Sai-gon in her gown,___ I made Queen of the town.

They paid_ me twice, and

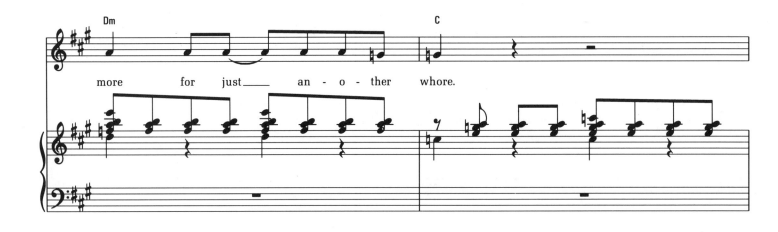

more for just_ an-o-ther whore.

Here I_ come U. S. A.,

your next_ champ's on his way. For men_ will al-ways be men,

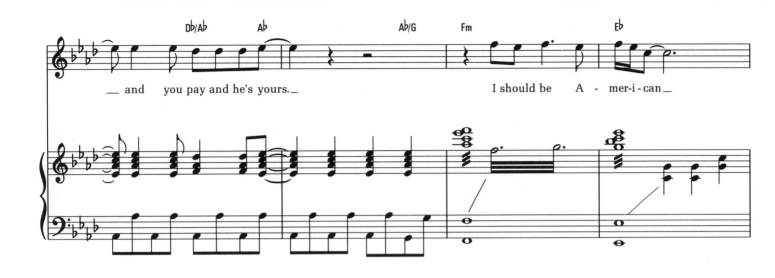

_ and you pay and he's yours._ I should be A - mer-i-can_

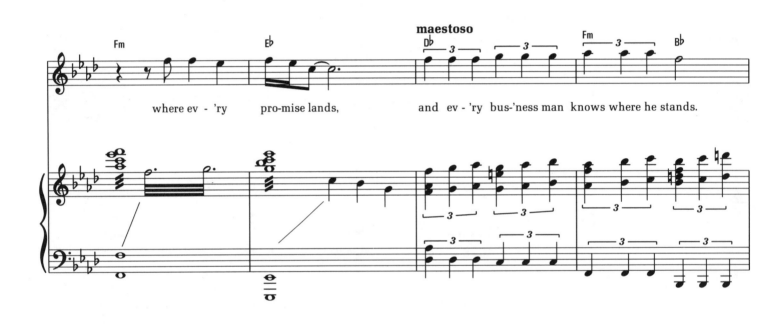

where ev - 'ry pro-mise lands, and ev - 'ry bus-'ness man knows where he stands.

maestoso

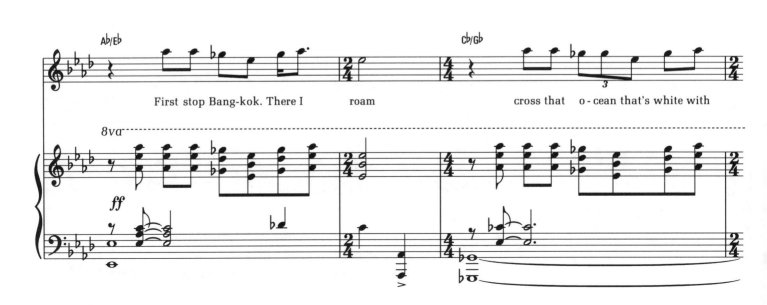

First stop Bang-kok. There I roam cross that o-cean that's white with

foam, to the place that's my heart's true home.

If you want to die in

bed don't care__ too much for coun-try.

I'd Give My Life
For You

Music by Claude-Michel Schönberg
Lyrics by Richard Maltby Jr. & Alain Boublil
Adapted from original French Lyrics by Alain Boublil

night,   when the stars burned like new   I knew what I must do.   I'll

give you____ a mil - lion things I'll nev - er own.   I'll

give you____ a world to con - quer when you're   grown.

You will be____ who you want to be.____   You   can choose what ev - er hea - ven

that made my bo - dy laugh and cry.____ Then by my side the proof I see,____

sub. *p*

molto rall.

his lit - tle one. Gods of the sun____ bring him to

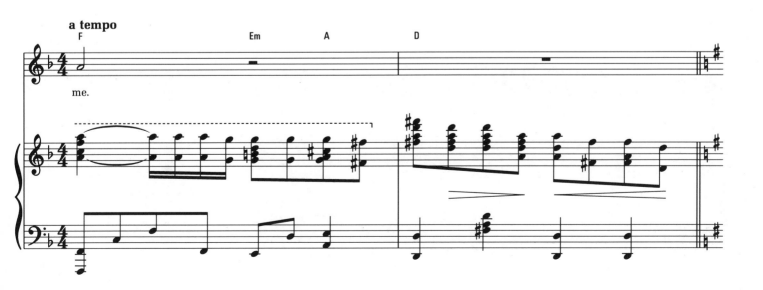

a tempo

me.

Bui-doi

Music by Claude-Michel Schönberg
Lyrics by Richard Maltby Jr. & Alain Boublil
Adapted from original French Lyrics by Alain Boublil

They are the fa-ces of— the chil-dren, the ones we left be-hind._____ They're called Bui-

-doi._____ The dust of life,_____ con-ceived in hell and born in

strife. They are the liv-ing re-min-der of all the good we failed to do. We can't for-

-get, must not for-got that they are all our— chil-dren too.

Those kids hit walls on ev'ry side, they don't be-long in a - ny place.__ Their his-t'ry they can't e-ven

hide, it's writ-ten__ on their face. I ne-ver thought one day I'd plead

__ for half-breeds from a land that's torn.__ But then I saw a camp__ for chil -

-dren, whose crime was be-ing born. They're called Bui - doi. The dust of

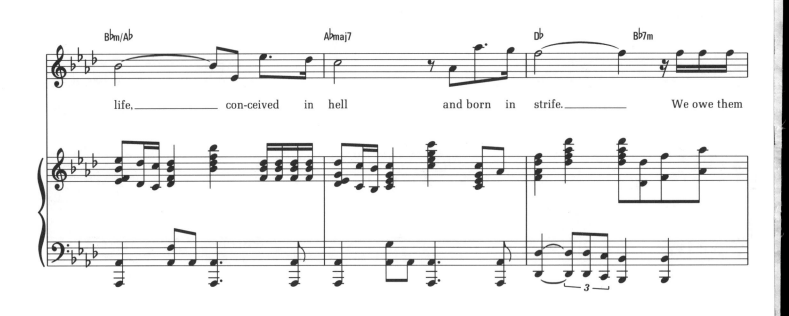

life, con-ceived in hell and born in strife. We owe them

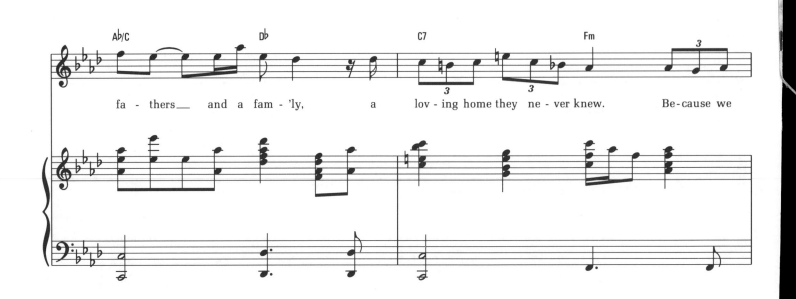

fa - thers and a fam - 'ly, a lov - ing home they ne - ver knew. Be-cause we

know deep in our hearts___ that they are all our___ chil-dren too.

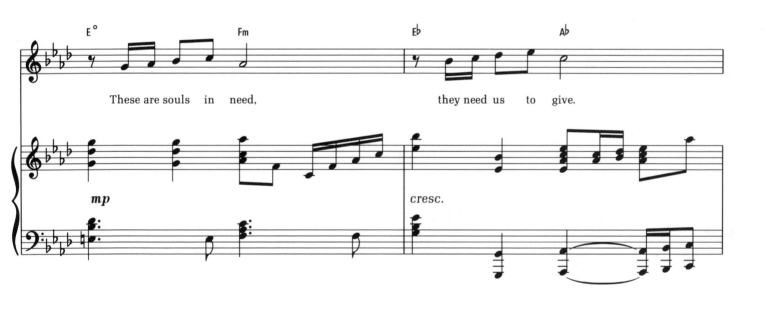

These are souls in need, they need us to give.

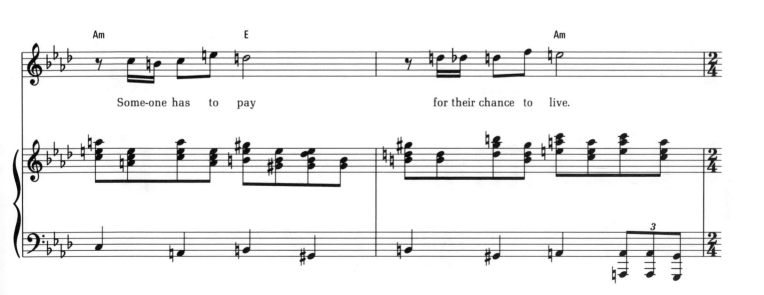

Some-one has to pay for their chance to live.

Now That I've Seen Her

Music by Claude-Michel Schönberg
Lyrics by Richard Maltby Jr. & Alain Boublil

Now that I've seen her I know why he lied, and I think it was

bet-ter when I did - n't know.

In her

eyes, in her voice, in the

heat_____ that filled the air part of him_____ still lin-gers there.

76

I know what pain her life to-day must be. But if it all comes down to

her or me, I won't wait, I___ swear___ I'll fight.

Now that I've seen her she's

more than a name   she is not some fling_ from long a - go._

Now that I've seen her I can't stay the same. Who's the man that I

al-ways trust-ed. Now I have to know._

The American Dream

Music by Claude-Michel Schönberg
Lyrics by Richard Maltby Jr. & Alain Boublil
Adapted from original French Lyrics by Alain Boublil

Make me Yan - kee, ___ they're my fam - i - ly.___ They're sel - ling what peo - ple

need. What's that I smell in the air, __ the A - mer - i - can dream.

Sweet as a new mil - lion - aire, __ the A - mer - i - can dream.

Pre - packed and rea - dy to wear,

the A-mer - i-can dream.

Bald peo - ple think they'll grow hair,___ the A-mer - i-can dream.

Call- girls are lin - ing Times Square, the A-mer - i-can dream.

Bums there have mo - ney to spare, _ the A-mer - i-can dream.

Cars that have bars take you there,

_ the A-mer - i-can dream.

On stage each night Fred As - taire,

_ the A-mer - i-can dream.

Schlitz down the drain,

pop the cham - pagne,

it's time we all en - ter - tain___ my A-mer - i - can dream.___

Bus- boys can buy the ho - tel,

11/02 (45876)